Prayer

The Still Place in the Storm

Ruthie Jacobsen

Pacific Press® Publishing Association
Nampa, Idaho
Oshawa, Ontario, Canada

Designed by Diane Baier

Printed in the United States of America

ISBN: 0-8163-1839-5

01 02 03 04 • 5 4 3 2

Acknowledgments

There are many who have contributed to this little book, and I want to recognize each contribution for what these thoughts and ideas have meant in my own life. Also for their help in the preparation of these materials.

Terry Tekyl, who wrote "A Mosquito on an Elephant's Rump," contributed tremendous plans and ideas for the chapter on the prayer room. He has written extensively in the field of prayer.

I am indebted to Bruce Wilkinson, for his wonderful little book, "The Prayer of Jabez," which is a faith-builder and an inspiration.

Gary Burns, chaplain and pastor at Dakota Adventist Academy, contributed the back cover—"God's Plans for You."

Diane Baier, my graphic artist, has the gift of making it look good, and doing it with patience and a smile.

My husband, my prayer-partner, my editor, and wordsmith, has been a great help in the preparation of these materials. He cheers me on.

Most of all, we acknowledge that prayer is God's gift to us. He has provided this connection with Heaven, and He is the One who is faithful to provide *the still places in the storm*.

Table of Contents

"Don't worry about anything; instead, pray about everything. Tell God what you need, and thank him for all he has done. If you do this, you will experience God's peace, which is far more wonderful than the human mind can understand. His peace will guard your hearts and minds as you live in Christ Jesus." *Philippians 4: 6 & 7 TPB**

Faith is a life -

committed beyond its means,

expecting what sense cannot certify,

based on God's promise,

depending on God's supply,

motivated for God's glory,

confident in God's integrity.

Ken Connolly - video "Obstacle to Comfort"

**Touch Point Bible*

Introduction

George Mueller, whose faith is an "obstacle to the comfort" of many Christians, lived by trusting in God, and in His promises. His prayers built five great stone buildings, orphanages, to house over 2000 children. These huge, quality buildings still stand in Bristol, England, and are being used today as a technical college.

Every day the children who lived there, their teachers, nurses, and house-parents were completely dependent on the providence of God in response to George Mueller's prayers.

He would ask no one but God for financial help, and over a period of 60 years, millions of dollars poured in for the care of the children. His prayers also provided support for many foreign missionaries and a host of Christian schools.

The children in his orphanages never missed a meal—the longest they ever had to wait for food was 30 minutes. Mueller's first goal was not to care for the children, but to prove that God is faithful, that He answers prayer.

During the Second World War, bombs fell heavily in Bristol, England, but the people discovered that the five Mueller buildings were somehow protected, and hundreds of them would run to one of these buildings, where they knew they would be safe.

Video - George Mueller, "Obstacle to Comfort" - The life of George Mueller

God still provides a place of stillness, of calm, in the storms of life. Prayer—time with God—is our place of calm, of safety. Solomon says in Proverbs 18:10:

> *"The name of the Lord is a strong tower; The righteous run to it and are safe."*

Whether it is your time of prayer each day, a day of prayer for you as an individual, or for your church, prayer—your meeting with God is life-changing. It is the place of refuge, of stillness, in the storms of life.

What are your Goals for a Day of Prayer?

1. Prayer -

The Day of Prayer is not an end in itself. This is a strategic time—at the beginning of each year, to refocus our priorities, to come together to pray and to allow God to re-excite us about what He wants to do in our lives and through us in the lives of others.

The first Sabbath of each new year has been designated as the North American Division Day of Prayer, but you may wish to plan others throughout the year for special events, such as school openings or evangelism.

Plan for prayer, intentional, for groups and/or individuals. Plan for prayer requests. Take time to listen and to pray for as many requests as possible. This draws your group together like nothing else can. Ask God for a bigger plan for prayer for your church.

Pray in and for your church. Small prayer groups may choose to meet in homes or at the church, asking God to be conspicuously present in the lives of family members, non-attending members, work associates, and others. The Lord has promised special wisdom as we pray and ask Him for it. *(James 1:5)*

2. Bible Study -

Provide opportunities for individual and group Bible Study.

On Friday night, or Sabbath afternoon, groups can meet at the church or in homes for Bible study and prayer together. There may be members of your church who are unable to worship with you on Sabbath, but would welcome someone or a small group to come and study and pray in their home or hospital room.

There are simple methods to follow, just using Scripture, that will provide spiritual growth and enhance maturity. God's Word applies to every situation and every need.

3. *Ministry* -

There are limitless resources to meet the needs and to reach others with the hope that we have been given in abundance. Be creative, as you respond to the leading of the Holy Spirit.

Prayerwalking—You may wish to plan a special time of prayerwalking on Sabbath morning, Friday night, or Sabbath afternoon. Pray in the baptistry, at the pulpit, in the pastor's study, the sanctuary, and each Sabbath School Division.

In Specific Places: If your church, for instance, is near a denominational entity, such as an academy, a college, a church school, or conference, union, or General Conference office, you may want to plan a regular time for prayerwalking there. In your planning, remember to prayerwalk for your own church on a regular basis.

> God often provides surprising interventions for His people as they follow this simple, but effective Old Testament method.

> A group from your church could plan to do this on a regular basis—once every week, or every month. What a difference this will make! And it will bring greater and more specific spiritual touches of His hand in your own life—as well as energizing the spiritual life of your prayerwalking group.

You may wish to especially pray for specific events—constituency meetings, special school events, meetings when special decisions will be made—for nominating committees and other groups.*

*For more specific information on prayerwalking, see *Prayerwalking—Praying On-Site With Insight*, by Steve Hawthorne, Creation House Publishers.

What would a Day of Prayer in your church look like?

There are probably a score of different ways it could be planned, and every one would be perfect for that church and it's needs. Here are just a few ways to look at your special day. These are ideas from pastors and churches where such plans are working well:

Friday night -

This is usually a family time. Think about family needs. Make this evening "family friendly." This provides a wonderful opportunity to reach out to single parents, and to all the family units in your parish. If you are planning to show a video, use one that would apply to families, or you could provide for baby-sitting, and something special for the children.

Friday night's meeting could be shorter, or an introduction to a longer meeting, so that families could leave earlier. Some churches plan an all-night prayer meeting, or a prayer time until 9 or 10 PM to allow for plenty of time for prayer requests and sharing of testimonies.

There are videos available at your ABC. Others could include:

"The Pastor's MVP" by John Maxwell—(offered without cost to pastors) 888-993-7847. This is a powerful resource, and one that your church will use and share. It could also be helpful in building bridges to pastors of other denominations in your community.

"The Power of a Song" by David Ring—615-771-9600. This is a sermon by an evangelist who has cerebral palsy. You will be blessed. It's message is a call to praise God and to sing.

"A House of Prayer" by James Cymbala—800-955-8746. This is one of the most powerful messages on prayer you will ever hear. It is scriptural, motivational, and inspirational.

Other activities for Friday night—to launch this special weekend, could include:

1. Praise music
2. Testimonies–answered prayer & praise
3. Prayer requests
4. Prayer times–silent prayer, prayer in twos, or groups.
5. Prayers of thanksgiving—not only for what He has done, but for what He will do.

Sabbath -

Some churches are beginning early—a group meets at the church (in some cases they may begin at 5 or 6 AM) to begin prayerwalking, or praying for specific needs for the day.

Sabbath School can be a time to again emphasize prayer, and to spend extra time in prayer in the classes.

In the afternoon, prayerwalking, or Bible study groups could meet. Many have found that there is something special about being together, praying for one another, for their church and community. God has promised to meet when even two or three come together in His name.

A special vespers might close the Sabbath hours. This could be a time for special prayer for the pastor or pastoral staff.

There are two special requests we continually bring to God in prayer:

1. Pray for our pastors, their spouses and families, and that God will show us how to hold them in "high regard" and to be supportive, as Paul explains in 1 Thess. 5:12 & 13.

2. The second area of need is for unity and harmony in the body of Christ. We are asking Him to bring down walls—between races, genders, and generations. He has promised that the Holy Spirit will bring unity.

Praying for the Worship Service

Many churches gather a group of believers to pray before the worship service, others have a group that meets to pray all through the service. Both groups seek to bathe the church's worship service in prayer, often using Scripture as the focus:

1. Psalm 80:1-3 - TPB
   "O God, enthroned above the cherubim, display your radiant glory ... Show us your mighty power. Come to rescue us. Turn us again to yourself, O God. Make your face shine down upon us. Only then will we be saved."

Pray that worshipers will sense God's presence and be in awe of His power, authority, love, wisdom and grace—that they will truly worship Him.

2. 1 Corinthians 2:2 - TPB
   "For I decided to concentrate only on Jesus Christ and his death on the cross."

Pray that all those present will know Jesus Christ as Savior and Lord and will grow to know Him better and better because of something in the worship service.

3. Ephesians 6:19, 20 - TPB
   "And pray for me too. Ask God to give me the right words as I boldly explain God's secret plan that the good news is for the Gentiles, too. . . . pray that I will keep on speaking boldly for him, as I should."

Pray for the pastor and/or speaker of the morning. Ask God to make His Word clear, and that it will be declared with boldness, love, and power.

4. Colossians 4:3 - TPB

   "Don't forget to pray for us, too, that God will give us many opportunities to preach about his secret plan—that Christ is also for you Gentiles."

Pray that there will be no distractions during the service that will keep God's people from focusing on Him and being fully open to the blessings He wants to pour into their lives.

5. 1 Timothy 2:1 - TPB

   "I urge you, first of all, to pray for all people. As you make your requests, plead for God's mercy upon them and give thanks."

Pray that all worship leaders—pastor, greeters, musicians, sound technicians, everyone participating in the service—will rely on and be used of the Lord.

6. James 1:22 - TPB

   "And remember, it is a message to obey, not just to listen to. If you don't obey, you are only fooling yourself."

Pray that worshipers will apply the biblical truths and principles they learn and will be encouraged, uplifted, rebuked, and challenged. Ask that the Holy Spirit will meet the needs of each one with the ability to carry out the truths throughout the week.

As your group meets together to plan for this Day of Prayer, expect something great because He has promised. Many of your members will find this a still place in the storm.

The Prayer Room

Jesus said, "My Father's house shall be a house of prayer." Didn't He mean that the primary activity in the local church should be to seek Him and that His will can then be accomplished in our congregations and communities?

The work of the prayer room is vital because this place becomes an upper room—a place of power. He meets with us as He has promised. Charles Spurgeon, the great English preacher, said that he could never preach or carry out his work of evangelism without his "powerhouse" which was a group of hundreds of people who were downstairs in the church praying while he preached.

The Prayer Room is not only important for a special event or occasion, but on an ongoing basis.

This becomes a special place where God's people come together to intercede in the vital work of the kingdom:

- for releasing the power of God in the church and its leadership
- reclaiming former members, and restoring broken lives
- lifting up the corporate experience of worship
- increasing the power and effectiveness of the spoken Word in worship

- supporting the work of God around the world
- bearing the burdens of the hurting
- for protection and for battling the powers of darkness
- for students leaving for school—for teachers as a new school year begins, and throughout the school year.

A special place set aside for prayer in your church or office can be a place of power for your family, your work, your church, your community.

The prayer room suggested here is a quiet place where continuous prayer can be offered in special times of need. In some places, there are prayer rooms that are continuous—around the clock, and every day of the week. This is made possible because members of the church have pledged themselves to a regular time to pray (for a specific time each week—such as 3-4 PM on Wednesdays), and are committed to keeping it.

Planning -

Prayer rooms vary—some are big, some are small, some are elaborate, some are more simple. They may vary in appearance as church buildings do, but many churches are making room to pray. Prayer room intercession is becoming a significant part of the life of the church in many places.

So what exactly, is a prayer room for your church? Even though they vary in appearance, there are several things prayer rooms do have in common:

- **They are private places.** Churches have found space for a prayer room in an extra classroom, unused office, junk room, empty storage closet, chapel–nearly any space that can be closed off from outside distractions.

- **They are comfortable places.** A prayer room should be an inviting place to sit, stand, or kneel before the Lord and enjoy His presence. Comfortable chairs, carpet, tables, plants, adequate lighting, good ventilation, pillows and wall hangings will help to create a pleasant place.

- **They are places of inspiration and information.** A globe or world map is helpful to remind those praying to pray big prayers for God's work around the world. Hymnbooks are helpful, a desk, and a simple filing system.

  Boxes or baskets are helpful to place requests to be prayed for, those requests that have been prayed for, and for answers to prayer. When someone enters the room with a specific request, they can go to the request cards and place their requests in the "Pray For" box.

When people come to the room to pray, they can go immediately to the request cards in the "Pray For" box, and bring these requests to God as they pray together. As each request is prayed for, that card can be transferred to the "Prayed For" box. When the first box is empty, the cards can be taken out of the "Prayed For" box and placed back into the "Pray For" box to begin again.

The box or basket with the answers becomes a very special and popular spot in the room. This is a place of encouragement and a place of prayers of thanksgiving. This strengthens faith and encourages and inspires further praying.

Bibles, books, articles on prayer, can also be available—some should be part of the necessary work of the prayer room, and remain in the room—and some can be available to be taken and used as personal or church resources for prayer ministries.

A bulletin board for photos of students, missionaries, or global prayer initiatives is an excellent resource and visual reminder.

Advantages of Prayer Places:

The Prayer Room has biblical precedent. The Upper Room was the place where the early church prayed continually (Acts 1:14). Around the clock they were there seeking God. In Acts 6:13 we find the apostles going to "the place of prayer." Apparently the early church had places for frequent and intense prayer.

Some Advantages to Establishing a Prayer Room:

1. **This makes it possible to schedule intentional prayer.** Quite often, if we don't schedule prayer, it won't happen.

2. **It provides a place where information can be gathered and displayed.** The assortment of information in a prayer room can help intercessors pray effectively and creatively. It provides a place where people can be united in their praying.

3. **A Prayer Room makes a statement to the church and community about the importance of prayer.** It can be a visible reminder to those who have needs that someone cares and is willing to pray for God's intervention.

4. **A Prayer Room provides a place to record the answers of God so that we do not forget to thank Him and praise Him for His faithfulness.** There is nothing that inspires people to keep praying, as uniting with other believers to see real-life answers.

5. **This is a place where prayer can be practiced and matured.** God has promised to meet with His people and to guide and instruct us as we get still before Him. The information provided in a prayer room can teach good prayer habits. Some prayer rooms encourage children to come and pray with their parents. This can be a wonderful experience of growth for more than one generation.

6. **A prayer room is inclusive.** Anyone can sign up to pray. It can be an inviting place for the elderly—who may have more time than others—or for young people, and business- men and women. It offers prayer opportunities and experiences for both new Christians and seasoned intercessors.

7. **A prayer room becomes a "hearing aid" for leaders of the church.** Just as Jesus did, pastors and church leaders need time and a place to draw apart and listen to God. He gives direction to those who wait patiently in His presence. The more time we spend with Him, the more He instills His heart in us.

8. **A prayer room provides a setting where major concerns are "bathed" in prayer.** It may be a big decision, a terminal illness, a major crisis, a special need or project—all require heavy doses of long-term prayer. These concerns can receive ongoing attention from intercessors.

9. **A prayer room ministers the presence of God in a special way to those who come.** One of the favorite songs sung in the Toronto Prayer Room at the General Conference Session in July, 2000, was "We Are Standing on Holy Ground." There was a sense of God's presence in that room. In a society full of noise and distractions of every kind, a prayer room provides a quiet place where the Holy Spirit can work and be heard, *a still place in the storm*.

10. **A prayer room is a control center for strategic prayer evangelism, and other prayer efforts.** It can serve as headquarters for a prayer plan during evangelism. As people come together to pray, they often take ownership of the church's vision to reach the city for Christ. In this way, the battle is not left to a few or to the pastor or evangelist alone. Scripture tells us that corporate repentance and seeking will invite revival and spiritual power. *2 Chron. 7:14*

Getting Started -

1. **Pray.** Ask your pastor, church prayer coordinator, or prayer committee to meet to ask for God's wisdom and presence in planning and preparing the church family for this step.

2. **Select a small group as "scouts."** Delegate the work of finding just the right place, to a few motivated members.

3. **Decide on the place.** When the room has been determined, plan the appointments carefully. Make sure there is adequate ventilation, lighting, and accessibility any hour of the day.

4. **Involve the church.** When it's time for wallpapering, painting, etc., involve as many people as possible. This also provides additional information for donated necessary items, and takes advantage of the creativity and abilities of many.

5. **Grand Opening.** Make this an event that the church will remember. Provide tours after church through the room, explaining the prayer boxes and providing answers to questions. This will open the way for more people to become involved in prayer ministries.

6. **A small group has continual responsibility.** This ensures upkeep, staffing when necessary, and communication to the church of needs and answers to prayer.

7. **Inform others—beyond the membership.** There may be occasions when others in the community may want to join you for special times of prayer—times of disaster, of national crisis, or local needs.

8. **Make your prayer room a place of hope.** "May the God of hope grant that our families, and church families may overflow with hope and hopefulness by the power of the Holy Spirit." *(from Romans. 15:13)*

Continuous Prayer
- over 24 hours or longer:

1. Team leaders will be needed for specific blocks of time (two to four hours is suggested).

2. Give the leaders a recommended plan to follow:

   A. Allow a short time for getting acquainted. In a large or multi-church setting, name tags may be helpful.

   B. Encourage prayer requests, before or during the prayer time. Keep this time brief so that large segments of time aren't taken up talking about prayer, rather than praying together.

   C. Share something briefly from Scripture. You may wish to ask groups to form for prayer and a short time of Bible study.

   D. What is the major focus for prayer, or specific need? Each hour come back to this special request.

   E. Keep a Prayer Request Box or basket available for "drop-ins" who may wish to request special intercession.

   F. There may be someone there who would like to share a short testimony. Keep these short, but they can also provide significant perspectives for prayer.

   G. Begin and close your prayer time with praise and singing. Short songs are always appropriate—even during prayer time.

3. This can be a great opportunity for all age groups, or Sabbath School Divisions to work together, or to take specific time slots in the schedule. Those who are physically unable to be present in the prayer room, can join in from home—perhaps with a speaker phone in the room. Let them know how much they are needed too.

Why plan for "Round the Clock" prayer?

Jesus has promised to be in our midst, even when only 2 or 3 come together to pray and He is faithful Who has promised. You experience something of what was told in Zechariah 8:21: "The inhabitants of one city shall go to another, saying, 'Let us continue to go and pray before the Lord, and seek the Lord of hosts.'"

Ellen White tells us (in PP, 509) "People of prayer are men and women of power." Little prayer provides little power; much prayer—much power. When special needs arise, the "much power" is also needed. Some churches schedule a 24-hr. prayer time once a month, or once a quarter.

Jesus said that His children will call out to Him—day and night.
Luke 18

Someone has said that if you want to do something for God, you form a committee, but if you want God to do something for you, you PRAY.

The Prayer of Jabez

There are some great prayers throughout Scripture. Some prayers, such as Solomon's prayer at the dedication of the temple—are long and profound. Others are short, but powerful.

The prayer of Jabez is a short, but very significant prayer, tucked away in a list of genealogies in the 4th chapter of 1 Chronicles. This is a very unlikely place to be looking for a prayer. The genealogy list is interrupted by this brief story, and then back to the lists.

1 Chronicles 4: 10 says: "And Jabez called on the God of Israel saying, 'Oh, that You would bless me indeed, and enlarge my territory, that your hand would be with me, and that You would keep me from evil, that I may not cause pain!' So God granted him what he requested."

A simple and short prayer with giant results. Many people have taken this short prayer as their own and use it daily. They discover that God loves to hear His Word in prayer, and the prayer of Jabez becomes their own powerful prayer of faith.

1. **Bless me indeed.** Bless me a lot—immeasurably, and undeniably. I need you, Lord. While on others Thou art calling, don't pass me by. Some of our prayer time can and should be prayers for ourselves. It is God's nature to give and to bless. This prayer fulfills His desire to answer.

2. **Oh, that you would enlarge my territory!** We can live larger lives for Him. His plans are much bigger than we could ever imagine. He tells us *(Ephesians 3:20)*, that His plans are greater than we could think or ask for. He wants to enlarge, expand everything He has given you to do for Him.

3. **Oh, that Your hand would be with me!** It is only accomplished by His strength, His power, His wisdom. Martin Luther reminded God at the beginning of his prayer that he was human, needy, weak, helpless, and unworthy. He wants us to ask. This is a prayer for guidance.

4. **Oh, that You would keep me from evil!** Bruce Wilkinson says, "God will not make you great, He becomes great in and through you." He has a strategy for sustaining a blessed life. It is His protective shield around you. He wants to remove the sin that can break the cycle of abundant living and provide peace and power.

God said that Jabez was more honorable than his brothers. We don't know very much about him, except that he prayed this prayer.

Why not covenant with God to pray this prayer daily for 60 days and just see how God wants to work in your life—to bless you, to enlarge your effectiveness, to provide new power and protection.

Creativity
in the Praying Church

You may find creative ideas generated right in your own congregation —here are a few as beginners:

Drive-Through Prayer

Russell Blair has initiated "Drive-Through-Prayer" at the Elementary School in Tranquility, New Jersey. Every Friday morning as parents drop their children off at school, he is there in the parking lot to pray with any who request it. Russell has found that this is also a powerful interdenominational ministry.

Mr. Blair says, "People everywhere are finding more and more things available at 'drive-throughs.' We now have drive-through banking, fast foods, cleaners, and pharmacies. Why not provide a place for drive-through prayer? Just a place to pause a minute and reach out to another person or family, and to pray for special needs. Parents request special prayer for their children at exam time, and other times of stress in their lives."

As a driver pulls out into the area provided, Russell walks over to the car—sometimes with an umbrella—takes requests, and prays.

"It's good to know that they can share these needs and know that someone will pray with and for them," Mr. Blair says. Here is a simple, yet effective and much-appreciated way to minister to those of our own church family, and of other faiths, whose children attend an SDA elementary school or academy.

Praying for the local police

What would happen if your church started praying for specific criminals, specific victims, and for the police in your city? This is unselfish and effective intercession that reaches out to the hurting.

Prayerwatch was started by Christian police officer Alan Stuart, in Nottingham, England. It has gained widespread support among churches. Police ask for prayers for specific incidents, but withhold the names of those involved. Christians have prayed for problems of theft, vandalism, and mistreatment of senior citizens.

Prayer requests are mentioned and dealt with during the regular worship services and later by individuals at home.

They have documented a reduction in crime as a result of the prayers of caring Christians in the community. Now they're beginning to find there are police officers who aren't Christians, who are cooperating, and initiating or passing on requests for prayer. It's making a difference; prayers not only create a still place in the storm, but can often calm the storm.

Prayers for public and private schools

Your church can make a difference on campuses. Partner with your school by providing volunteers who can listen to problems and pray. Pray for educators—for all school personnel—from your congregation or home. Pray for your school board during their meetings. Pray about each agenda item.

Encourage the formation of Christian clubs at nearby school campuses.

Encourage "Closet Ministry" for senior citizens

The early church knew the secret of overcoming obstacles through the glorious weapon of prayer. They seemed to live by the Throne. There is an urgent need today for believers everywhere to "stand in the gap" and to pray for the pastor, teachers, church officers, evangelism, special needs, and for specific individuals.

Retirement, for many, brings a change of pace. "Closet Ministry" is a special time each day or each week that can be devoted to a prayer time, either as individuals or groups. This can make a difference that can only be measured in eternity. Shut-ins, invalids, and those with various disabilities are finding new vistas where they can serve and serve powerfully.

Arms around the world

How can we break through the darkness in the least evangelized nations of the world?

How can we strengthen the hands of our church leaders, pastors, and members in the 10/40 window, and every world Division?

The 10/40 window is a place so dark and so untouched by the efforts of evangelism that from a human standpoint, it is impossible to reach. This is a place where more than four billion people live who have virtually no access to the Gospel. This is where the poorest of the poor labor endlessly just to scratch out a meager existence, where famine has not only desecrated the land, but the minds, bodies, and spirits of the people. It is the seat where Satan has great power, and it has been called hell on earth.

This troubled area stretches from West Africa, through the Middle East to eastern Asia. More than 60 countries fall within the boundaries of 10 and 40 degrees latitude north of the equator. These are the most spiritually impoverished countries, which include the majority of Muslims, Hindus, and Buddhists in the world.

How can we get our arms around the world? How can the peoples of the 10/40 window be reached?

How can other countries, the sleeping countries of Europe and America—be awakened? In prayer we can ask God to intervene for His children—to strengthen His church, to provide laborers, means, faith, and power. We can ask Him to touch every nation, every tribe, every language, every person, with His love.

In prayer we can bond with the nations of the world for the harvest.

Christ promised that if we ask anything in His name, He will do it.
John 14:14

There is only one place in Scripture where Christ gave a problem, and then pointed out the solution:

> "Then He said to His disciples, 'The harvest truly is plentiful, but the laborers are few. Therefore pray the Lord of the harvest to send out laborers into His harvest.'" *Matthew 9:37 & 38*

Ellen White has this to say about reaching out to the other nations around us:

> "The home missionary work will be farther advanced in every way when a more liberal, self-denying, self-sacrificing spirit is manifested for the prosperity of foreign missions; for the prosperity of the home work depends largely, under God, upon the reflex influence of the evangelical work done in the countries afar off." *ChS 170*

> "Those who take up their appointed work will not only bless others, but will themselves be blessed. The consciousness of duty well done will have a reflex influence upon their own souls. The despondent will forget their despondency, the weak will become strong, the ignorant intelligent, and all will find an unfailing helper in Him who has called them." *CH 391*

When we reach out unselfishly to touch others for Christ, we are even more abundantly blessed.

Possibilities:

It will take a plan, it will take intentional, purposeful effort to accomplish this impossible task.

Maybe your church would like to "adopt" a specific world Division, or part of the 10/40 Window as a special focus for your prayers. Discuss this with your Prayer Committee. How would God want to enlarge your vision and the possibilities of great eternal consequences as a result? We may think that we are being creative and really serious about these thrilling prayer adventures, but our God is even more serious. He is the One Who is not willing that any should perish.

Biblical Strengths

to request for yourself & your children:

1. **Salvation.** "Lord, let salvation spring up that we may obtain the salvation that is in Christ Jesus, with eternal glory." *(Isa. 45:8, 2 Tim. 2:10)*

2. **Growth in grace.** "I pray that we may grow in the grace and knowledge of our Lord and Savior Jesus Christ." *(2 Peter 3:18)*

3. **Love.** "Grant, Lord, that we may learn to live lives of love, through the Spirit who dwells in us." *(Gal. 5:25, Eph. 5:2)*

4. **Honesty and Integrity.** "May integrity and honesty be our virtue and our protection." *(Ps. 25:21)*

5. **Self Control.** "Father, help us to be alert and self-controlled in all we do." *(1 Thess. 5:6)*

6. **Love for God's Word.** "May we grow to find Your Word more precious than much pure gold and sweeter than honey from the comb." *(Ps. 19:10)*

7. **Kindness.** "Lord, may we always try to be kind to each other and to everyone else." *(1 Thess. 5:15)*

8. **Generosity.** "Grant that we may be generous and willing to share, and so lay up treasure for ourselves as a firm foundation for the coming age."
(1 Tim.6:18, 19)

9. **Humility.** "God, please cultivate in us the ability to show true humility toward all." *(Titus 3:2)*

10. **Joy.** "May we be filled with the joy given by the Holy Spirit." *(1 Thess. 1:6)*

11. **Willingness and ability to work.** "Teach us, Lord, to value work and to work at it with all our hearts, as working for the Lord, not for men."
(Col. 3:23)

12. **Prayerfulness.** "Grant, Lord, that our lives will be marked by prayerfulness, that we may learn to pray in the Spirit on all occasions with all kinds of prayer and requests." *(Eph. 6:18)*

13. **Passion for God.** "Lord, please instill in us each a soul that 'followeth hard after thee' (Ps. 63:8 KJV), one that clings passionately to you."

14. **Gratitude.** "Help us to live lives that are always overflowing with thankfulness and always giving thanks to God the Father for everything, in the name of our Lord Jesus Christ." *(Eph. 5:20, Col. 2:7)*

15. **Faith.** "I pray that faith will find root and grow in our hearts, that by faith we may gain what has been promised to us."
(Luke 17:5,6 & Heb. 11: 1-40)

Family Prayers

What happens when a family prays together? What's the atmosphere of "family worship"? Picture a little family together before the children leave for school. They pray together, taking the Word of God as their assurance, and asking God to put His hedge about each one throughout the day. Parents can know that He will keep His word, and His arms will be about their children.

Teri & Tedd have established this as a daily practice, and have been rewarded and given the assurance that those things just beyond their grasp—the tangible and intangible situations in the lives of their precious little ones, Jessica and Jordan—are safe in the hands of their Father. They have also seen that His rewards come in the characters reflected in their children.

Ask the Macey family what happens when a family prays and trusts God for one another. Fred was just 17, young, strong, athletic, and had just come in that morning in September, from jogging. His sister Martha heard the door open, and then a thud as Fred hit the floor. She ran to find his crumpled body by the front door—he was totally unresponsive. He was rushed to the hospital where physicians worked feverishly over him to discover the problem. Fred, at 17, had had a stroke! Not just a minor problem, but a massive stroke, followed by others, until he had to be placed on life-support equipment which breathed for him.

Fred's carotid artery was occluded, blocking the blood supply to his brain. He couldn't breathe, speak, see, or even think. As his physicians worked, the family prayed, and were soon joined by others there in the town of Berrien Springs, Michigan where they live.

Others far and near began praying as they heard the news of the tragedy in the Macey family.

After more than two weeks, the physicians came to Dorothy and Epifanio, Fred's parents, with the words they had been dreading. "There is no sign of any brain activity. I'm afraid we'll have to stop the life support, because Fred is gone."

Before the ventilator was turned off, the Macey family met one last time in the little chapel, again pleading with God to save their boy. Only the parents were allowed in the hospital room as the tubes were removed. The physicians took out the endotracheal tube that had been in place to keep oxygen flowing into his lungs, and as they pulled out the tube, "Epi," Fred's father, couldn't stand still another second. He pushed past the others working around his son's bed. Rushing to Fred's side, he grabbed his shoulders, and said, "Fred, are you going to die? Please let God prove His power." Fred opened his eyes. He began breathing on his own for the first time in three weeks! The Great Physician was there.

Dorothy looked at her son in amazement and said, "Fred, what would you like?" He smiled, as he said, "I'd like water." What rejoicing! What a dramatic answer to prayer. Fred still had a long road ahead. Now, several years later, his speech is still minimal, but he can walk—with a slight limp, and he can sing one song—"Amazing Grace." He sings the song with emotion, and with all the understanding of his experience. "Amazing Grace, how sweet the sound that saved a wretch like me. I once was lost, but now am found, was blind, but now I see."

His determination and rehabilitation have also been a miracle of God's grace, and he and his family share his story everywhere in their attempt to try to thank their God for the miracle to their family.

The Macey family has been a praying family from the beginning. Sometimes Martha chafed a little over the "rules" of her family. Everyone had to be dressed for worship before breakfast—every morning. But now she realizes the power in this practice that she sometimes thought was only a ritual.

What happens when the larger family of God prays together? Throughout Scripture the answer is given. We sometimes miss the beginning of God's stories. We remember the wonderful deliverance, or miracle, but may not begin at the very beginning of the story—where God's people are in prayer, and often in prayer and fasting. They come to Him because they know that there is no other place to go. But they also know that there is nothing impossible with Him.

In fact, there was no word for impossible in the Hebrew language because God's family knew there was nothing He would not or could not do if they were asking Him and if it was His will. His covenant with them covered all of that.

Does it make a difference? Ask Peter. He was in jail—handcuffed to guards—the situation looked hopeless, but his church family was praying. Angels were sent in answer to prayer, and soon Peter was free!

What would happen today if our prayers were multiplied–and really creating more and more "violence" in heaven? Matthew 11:12 tells us that "the kingdom of heaven suffers violence, and the violent take if by force." Then in the little book *That I May Know Him* p. 272, that text is given wonderful illumination. It says that it doesn't mean that we are to become emotionally worked up with some power of our own, but if we are faithful in earnest prayer, that is actually interpreted in heaven as violence. Our prayers for each other—in the family of God can cause a stir in heaven!

The prayers of children reach heaven—in fact, Jesus said that we all need to have that kind of simple trust and faith in His faithfulness. What would happen in your life, in your family, and in your church, if your theme song were:

"Great is Thy Faithfulness, O God, my Father,
There is no shadow of turning with Thee.
Thou changest not, Thy compassions, they fail not,
As Thou hast been, Thou forever wilt be.

Great is Thy faithfulness. Great is Thy faithfulness,
Morning by morning, new mercies I see.
All I have needed, Thy hand hath provided,
Great is Thy faithfulness, Lord, unto me.

The prayers of God's children are heard in heaven, and are a joy to His heart. Little Sarah, age 8, said it this way:

"Dear God, I love you. I just want to let you know ahead of time that I'd like to be there with you in heaven.
Love Always, Sarah"

Alexis said, "Dear God, What do you do with families that don't have much faith? There's a family on the next block like that. I don't want to get them in trouble. I don't want to say who. See you in church."
Alexis, age 9

We may smile at the prayers of our children, but we are also touched by their simplicity, trust, and direct honesty. These are the qualities children bring to prayer, and they bring a depth of intimacy with God that may surprise many adults. Children have an intuitive awareness of God, and they are quick to respond to God with trust, awe, and love.

Have you ever wondered what God would do if you and others in God's family came together around His Word just to develop that greater awareness of Him and to pray together?

Have you ever wondered what would happen in your life, in your family, or in your church, if you and your family were more aware of God's presence and His goodness—if you were more confident of what He could and would do for you.

> "It is not the capabilities you now possess or ever will have that will give you success. It is that which the Lord can do for you. We need to have far less confidence in what man can do and far more confidence in what God can do for every believing soul. He longs to have you expect great things from Him."
>
> *COL 146*

When God's people come together in faith, in support of one another, and in agreement in prayer, He has pledged Himself to do wonderful things. Over and over Paul asked his fellow Christians, who were his "children," to pray for him. He called them "saints" even though he was often concerned about them and knew that they needed counsel.

What would happen if we declared a moratorium on all criticism in our families and church families, and determined to come together often in prayer and agreement—seeing each other as "saints," claiming God's promises for one another, and praying for our pastors and church leadership? Our time is short, the combined prayers of God's people are needed now more than ever before.

If you are young, God needs your energetic prayers of trust; if you are an adult, He needs your prayers of need and love. If you are in your sunset years you may have more prayer power than anyone because your time can be devoted to prayer now more than ever.

There has never been a revival in history that was not preceded by the united and sustained prayers of God's people. As His people come together now to pray for one another, for pastors, church leaders, for revival, for a new usefulness, He has committed Himself to making us ready for His coming. He Himself will see to it that we have many others who will go with us and will thank us for our prayers that helped to build for them *a still place in the storm*.

A Four-wheeled Love Story

The first car I ever owned was an old Ford. A very old Ford. In fact, it was older than I was. I needed a way to get to school and to work so I started shopping for something I could afford. I finally found it. An "elderly" Ford with lots of experience.

Earlier in its life it had been black, but now it was hard to tell. There were huge cracks in the wooden floor board, springs stuck out through the front seat cushion. The left front tire was so worn you could see the inner tube (remember those?), and the horn didn't work. But that really didn't matter because it had no muffler.

I remember my mother's first words the afternoon I drove up in front of the house. She asked, "Did anyone see you driving it?"

But I loved that car. I found some black paint in the garage and painted it. I know it looked as though it had been done with a broom, but at least it was all the same color now. I found some well-worn carpet for the floor, covered the seat with a blanket, and bought a used tire. Oh, and I found an old muffler. Although it didn't quite fit, it did make the car run a bit quieter.

The day actually came when my mother rode with me. A short trip, it's true, but there she was, riding in my car. When we got back home she said, "Well, that wasn't so bad." But you see, to me that little old Ford was beautiful for two reasons—it was mine, and I could see it for what it would become.

Fortunately, God looks at us the same way. He doesn't see the damage caused by life's road, or our blemishes and scars. He sees us as already beautiful, transformed by His skilled hand. I once heard a parable of a man who had lost his way and lived a life of rebellion. As he neared the end of his life he seemed to hear Satan saying, "Who wants you … ? Look at the mess you've made of your life." But then he heard unmistakably clear the voice of God whisper, "I'll take you!"

That's the kind of God He is. We're His because He bought us, and then set about to make us beautiful. And at whatever stage of restoration you are today, remember that in God's sight, you are beautiful. He sees you for what you are becoming. The God who loves to restore broken things—that's our God. A Day of Prayer is a wonderful time to re-connect, or to especially devote extra time to listen for His voice in the little and big things in our lives, and to realize that He does really value us.

Don Jacobsen